The Compassion of the Almighty

"*All humanity finds shelter in the shadow of Your wings. Psalm 36:7b*

Rachel Laurn

Copyright © 2014 by Rachel Laurn

The Compassion of the Almighty
by Rachel Laurn

Printed in the United States of America

ISBN 9781498401593

All rights reserved solely by the author. The author guarantees all contents are original and do not infringe upon the legal rights of any other person or work. No part of this book may be reproduced in any form without the permission of the author. The views expressed in this book are not necessarily those of the publisher.

Scripture quotations taken from the New Living Translation (NLT). Copyright © 1996, 2004, 2007 by Tyndale House Foundation. Used by permission. All rights reserved.

www.xulonpress.com

Foreword

So often, those who are not actively walking with Jesus Christ or even those who are, are at a loss, especially during difficult times, to find the right scripture at the right time, to help you in your time of need. As a result, the Bible stays on the shelf.

This is a book you can reach for to get you started.

It will give you what you need right now, and then, once you have found where you want to be, grab your Bible and dig deeper.

Where in the Bible does it actually say that God loves me? Turn to Chapter One and find numerous scriptures declaring God's love for you. Do you need direction in your life? Chapter Three shows you that God has a plan for your life and He is directing it! Are you worried? Chapter 4 is entitled "Do Not Worry"! It contains "worry" scriptures!

The chapters begin with the details of the author's struggle with an incurable, debilitating disease called Multiple Sclerosis (MS). But as you will see, she discovers, as you will, how to rise above the ashes through faith in the Creator of the Universe, the Master of Everything. You will see how God can turn evil and pain and distress into Victory and Blessing and Glory.

You will begin to grasp how a Powerful, Almighty God can have such compassion and tenderness for His loved ones. You will develop an INTIMATE relationship, a personal friendship, with the Great "I AM". You will begin to abide underneath the arms of the Everlasting King of kings.

The chapters end with counsel from God, devotion with the Almighty, and encouragement directly from scripture. I encourage you to dwell here, pray here, write down your innermost thoughts in the spaces provided. This is where we rise from the ashes. This is where we soar with eagles in the heavens.

Introduction

Please be assured that all of God's promises are true and can be depended on.

"Your promises have been thoroughly tested; that is why I love them so much." Psalm 119:140 (NLT). **"Every word of God proves true."** Proverbs 30:5a (NLT).

The writer of Hebrews testifies that **"the Word of God is full of living power. It is sharper than the sharpest knife, cutting deep into our innermost thoughts and desires..."** Hebrews. 4:12 (NLT).

We can be assured that: **"Such things were written in Scripture long ago to teach us. They give us hope and encouragement as we wait patiently for God's promises."** Romans 15:4 (NLT).

Walk with me through the pages of God's love. He is anxious for you to see all that He has for you and wants for you and how precious you are to Him.

Once you can begin to grasp the immense love and caring and compassion of our God, you will then be so overwhelmed with love and awe and thanksgiving, you will WANT to do whatever you can to please the One Who carries you through life. In doing this, you will begin to experience a fulfilled Christian life, wrapped up in the arms of God Himself!

"We throw open our doors to God and discover at that same moment that He has already thrown open His door to us. We find ourselves standing where we always hoped we might stand–out in the wide open spaces of God's grace and glory, standing tall and shouting our praise." Romans 5:2 (Msg.)

What a privilege! What a blessing! God loves you and is caring for you and listening to you. He wants to be your friend! Take His hand!

Table of Contents

Foreword v
Introduction vii

Chapter 1 11
   I LOVE YOU **13**

Chapter 2 18
   Talk To Me **19**

Chapter 3 23
   I Have a Plan for Your Life **25**

Chapter 4 29
   Please Don't Worry **31**

Chapter 5 36
   I Will Help You **38**

Chapter 6 43
   I Don't Want You to be Afraid **45**

Chapter 7 50
   I Will Stay Right by Your Side **52**

Chapter 8 55
   Trust Me in Times of Trouble **57**

Chapter 9 61
   I Will Protect You **62**

Endnotes 67

Chapter 1

"Behold, I have inscribed you on the palms of My hands..." Isaiah 49:16a (NASB). **I have...hidden you safe within my hand..."** Isaiah 51:16 (NASB)

I always thought I was going to grow up and things would be okay. I wanted to be "normal". You never think bad things are going to happen in your life. How could you? Our human nature just expects everything to be alright.

I got married in 1986. I had two kids in 1988 and 1989. I earned a degree as a Paralegal at a community college in 1991, and was hired at a major law firm in Phoenix, Arizona in 1992. Things were looking like I had always dreamed. It was hard for me to believe that I really made something of myself and had a career of my very own. I was "normal"! Until 1999....

My double vision was so bad, I could hardly see. I needed help getting to work and I needed the walls to guide me down the halls. My body was so stiff, I could barely move. I was so dizzy, I felt the need to keep my eyes closed. I had trouble walking straight. I had no balance and I could not keep a hold of anything. Everything I touched, I dropped. Even when I tried really hard to hang onto things, my fingers just were not communicating with each other. I needed prescriptions to sleep at night. My motor skills were not working properly. When I did try to drive, my foot would slam on the gas and the brake and cause the car to jolt back and forth. I was so embarrassed. I couldn't imagine what the problem was.

I had a nervous breakdown at one point. There was about a week that I could not go outdoors. I did not go to work. I did not fathom how I would pick up the kids from school, and I could not be alone for one minute. I cried from the time I woke up until I finally fell asleep at night. My husband took care of the kids and made the meals and he sat with me day and night. He rubbed my body from my head to my feet because I was so stiff. I didn't know what was happening. I cried out to God for help! I kept asking, "What is happening? Where are You? I can't see You. What have I done? Is this punishment, is it planned, have You gone away? Tell me what to do!"

O Lord...Rescue me...Bend down and listen to me;...Be for me a great rock of safety;...for you have seen my troubles, and You care about the anguish of my soul...Have mercy on me, Lord, for

I am in distress. My sight is blurred because of my tears...in Your unfailing love, save me... Psalm 31:1,2,7,9,16 (NLT).

I went to a neurologist, an ophthalmologist, an ENT doctor, an internal medicine doctor, and my regular doctor. I went to one of the best neurologists in the country at Barrows Neurological Institute. The fabulous diagnosis I received was stress and anxiety! They gave me an anti-depressant and sent me home. I kept questioning–who has double vision with stress? I thought maybe I had missed that medical class somehow and I took the meds he gave me. This "attack" lasted from April to September. I had no idea that one day I would be told that I had Multiple Sclerosis (MS).

Journal Entry: November 11, 1999: ...There was a point I was so stressed, that I was seeing double vision. I was dizzy, weak, couldn't drive, couldn't walk straight. I didn't have balance, I needed prescription drugs to sleep at night. It got so bad, I had an MRI done on my brain. I went to numerous doctors and spent thousands of dollars to find out that it was totally stress and anxiety. I am getting better now although I still need help to sleep at night...

I had had a terrible MS attack at a time when I did not know I had MS.

(Multiple sclerosis (MS) is an incurable, potentially debilitating disease in which your body's immune system eats away at the protective sheath that covers your nerves. Damage to the nerves causes a disruption in the communication between your brain, spinal cord and other areas of your body. This condition may result in deterioration of the nerves themselves, a process that's not reversible.

Symptoms vary widely, depending on the amount of damage and the nerves that are affected. People with severe cases of multiple sclerosis may lose the ability to walk or speak clearly. Other symptoms include:

- Numbness or weakness in one or more limbs
- Double vision, blurring of vision, or potentially loss of vision
- Tingling or pain in parts of your body
- Tremor, lack of coordination or unsteady gait
- Fatigue
- Dizziness
- Loss of balance
- Cognitive issues

Multiple sclerosis can be difficult to diagnose early in the course of the disease because symptoms often come and go — sometimes disappearing for months.

Devotion

I LOVE YOU

"Do not be afraid, for I have ransomed you.
I have called you by name; you are mine.
When you go through deep waters, I will be with you.
When you go through rivers of difficulty, you will not drown.
When you walk through the fire of oppression, you will not be burned up;
the flames will not consume you.
For I am the Lord, your God, the Holy One of Israel, your Savior....
because you are precious to Me.
You are honored, and I love you."
Isaiah 43:1-4 (NIV)

Grasping God's love is a life-changing experience.

"Your beauty and love chase after me every day of my life."
Psalm 23:6 (Msg).

"O Lord, You have examined my heart and know everything about me.
You know when I sit down or stand up. You know my every thought when far away.
You chart the path ahead of me and tell me where to stop and rest.
Every moment you know where I am.
You know what I am going to say even before I say it, Lord.
You both precede and follow me. You place your hand of blessing on my head.
Such know ledge is too wonderful for me, too great for me to know!"
How precious are your thoughts about me, O God!
They are innumerable! I can't even count them; they outnumber the grains of sand!
And when I wake up in the morning, you are still with me!"
Psalm 139:1-6, 17,18 (NLT)

"God sure loves us! He thinks about us all the time and delights in taking care of us. I wish I could mail you a handful of sand today and have you hold it in your hands while you try to count the grains! It is estimated there are at least 40 million, trillion grains of sand on earth — that, according to God's Word, can only begin to portray how much He loves us!" [1]

"Your unfailing love, O Lord, is as vast as the heavens,
Your faithfulness reaches beyond the clouds.
Your righteousness is like the mighty mountains,
Your justice like the ocean depths.
You care for people and animals alike, O Lord, how precious is Your unfailing love, O God!
All humanity finds shelter in the shadow of Your wings.
You feed them from the abundance of Your own house,
letting them drink from Your rivers of delight.

For You are the fountain of life, the light by which we see."
Psalm 36:5-9 (NLT)

**"For Your unfailing love is as high as the heavens.
Your faithfulness reaches to the clouds."**
Psalm 57:10 (NLT)

"Nothing could ever make God love you more or less than He loves you right now,
because He loves you 100%, 100% of the time!" 2

"God is love."
I John 4:8, 16 (NIV)

"In Your generous love, I am really living at last!" Psalm 63:3 (Msg.)

**"He has dressed us with salvation as if it were our clothes.
He has put robes of godliness on us.
We are like a groom who is dressed up for his wedding.
We are like a bride who decorates herself with her jewels."**
Isaiah 61:10 (NIV)

Knowing we are loved by God every minute of the day can give us the courage to face every circumstance.

"... His love endures forever."
Jeremiah 33:11b (NIV)

"God doesn't love us because we're important, we're important because God loves us!" 3

"...having loved His own who were in the world, He loved them to the end." John 13:1b (NAS.).
"For He loves us with unfailing love; the faithfulness of the Lord endures forever."
Psalm 117:2 (NLT)

**"And I am convinced that nothing can ever separate us from His love.
Death can't and life can't. The angels can't, and the demons can't.
Our fears for today, our worries about tomorrow,
and even the powers of hell can't keep God's love away.
Whether we are high above the sky or in the deepest ocean,
nothing in all creation will ever be able to separate us from the love of God
that is revealed in Christ Jesus our Lord."**
Romans 8:38, 39 (NLT)

**"...we can't round up enough containers to hold everything
God generously pours into our lives through the Holy Spirit."**
Romans 5:5 (Msg.)

As children of an Almighty God, we are blessed to have such a generous and loving Dad!

> **"No good thing will the Lord withhold from those who do what is right.**
> **O Lord Almighty, happy are those who trust in You."**
> Psalm 84:11b, 12 (NIV)

"...as a bridegroom rejoices over his bride, so will your God rejoice over you." Isaiah 62:5b (NIV).
"For your Maker is your husband–the Lord Almighty in His name." Isaiah 54:5a (NIV)

God's love did not begin at the cross. It began in eternity, before the clock of civilization began to move.

> **"...Your unfailing love is higher than the heavens.**
> **Your faithfulness reaches to the clouds."**
> Psalm 108:4 (NLT)

> **"I'm praying that the Lord Jesus guide our hearts**
> **into an ever deeper understanding of His love.**
> **Then, we will be able to take in with all Christians**
> **the extravagant dimensions of Christ's love.**
> **Reach out and experience the breadth! Test its length!**
> **Plumb the depths! Rise to the heights!**
> **Live full lives, full in the fullness of God."**
> Ephesians 3:18 (Msg.)

What a great and loving and extremely generous Master we have!
God's character is to give generously and without reproach.
James 1:5 says "...God, who gives generously to all and without reproach..."
This means that He does not resent us asking.
He gives without finding fault and He gives ungrudgingly.
There is no one who loves you like God loves you.

> **"For the Lord is good.**
> **His unfailing love continues forever,**
> **and His faithfulness continues to each generation."**
> Psalm 100:5 (NLT)

> **"See how very much our heavenly Father loves us,**
> **for He allows us to be called His children,**
> **and we really are!"**
> I John 3:1a (NLT)

We have a loving Father who cares deeply for His children.

> **"For the mountains may be removed and the hills may shake,**
> **but My loving-kindness will not be removed from you,**
> **And My covenant of peace will not be shaken,**
> **Says the Lord who has compassion on you."**
> Isaiah 54:10 (NAS)

Jesus is compassionate because He also felt sorrow, pain and hardship. He personally knows what we feel.

**"The Lord is compassionate and gracious,
slow to anger and abounding in loving-kindness."**
Psalm 103:8 (NAS)

**"Yet the Lord longs to be gracious to you,
He rises to show you compassion."**
Isaiah 30:18a (NIV)

From Genesis to Revelation, the Lord is reaching out to us.

**"I will bind you to Me forever with chains of righteousness
and justice and love and mercy.
I will betroth you to me in faithfulness and love,
and you will really know me then as you never have before."**
Hosea 2:19, 20 (LB)

"...may the Lord direct your hearts into the love of God..."
2 Thessalonians 3:5a (NAS)

Thoughts

Chapter 2

"My heart has heard you say, 'Come and talk with Me.' And my heart responds, 'Lord, I am coming.'" Psalm 27:8 (NLT)

The attack lasted five months. My bosses were very patient so I was able to keep my job and continue to work the best I could. I struggled and stumbled around, but I was determined to keep working. I had no idea what was going on with my body and definitely had no reason to believe I had an incurable, debilitating disease that would give me difficulty for the rest of my life.

I was convinced that if I started to eat right, exercise more, and take more vitamins, that things would soon be back to normal. Eventually, things did seem to get back to normal. I regained my vision and my balance, the dizziness began to fade away, and slowly, I began to feel well again. **"...I am the Lord who heals you."** Exodus 15:26b

It was during these months when God began to work on my soul. I began to feel His presence in my life, rather than just have knowledge of it. I look back on that time with great fondness and comfort. I had never felt the grace and compassion of God like I had during those months. It sounds crazy, but it's true. God was nearer to me than my own soul. They say the enormity of the ocean cannot be grasped until it is seen. Well, it is the same with God's love. You cannot fathom it until you actually experience it.

"When I pray, You answer me and encourage me by giving me the strength I need." Psalm 138:3 (LB)

I would not trade those times of my life for anything because it was then that I experienced God's power and grace and compassion in my life. I began to understand that *peace transcends circumstances*.

Journal Entry: March 15, 2000: I am feeling a lot better. I must have been eating too much junk food or something. I don't know what happened. I really thought I was losing it. I am 32 years old and thought I needed a wheelchair! Ha! I have got to start taking better care of myself. I didn't think I had to do that until my 40s...

Devotion

Talk To Me

The Lord listens to us through prayers and He talks to us through His Word.

"He listens the split second I call to Him."
Psalm 4:3b (Msg.)

God is not silent. The second person of the Trinity is called The Word. The Bible is the inevitable outcome of God's continuous speech.

**"I love the LORD because He hears and answers my prayers.
Because He bends down and listens,
I will pray as long as I have breath!"**
Psalm 116:1, 2 (NLT)

Experience the kindness of the Lord by reading His Word.

Prayer and the Word–ongoing conversation!

"I am praying to You because I know You will answer, O God."
Psalm 17:6a (NLT)

We don't twist God's arm in prayer, we grab a hold of what He already has and wants for us!

**"But in my distress I cried out to the Lord;
yes, I prayed to my God for help.
He heard me from His sanctuary;
my cry reached His ears."
Psalm 18:6 (NLT)**

"The Hebrew word for "distress" means "a stone in a narrow place". We all find ourselves in tight spots and can be assured that the Lord hears our cry for help and He will move heaven and earth to help us." 4

"I cried out to the Lord, and He answered me from His holy mountain."
Psalm 3:4 (NLT)

Prayer is an unbelievable opportunity! The God of the universe invites us to have fellowship and conversation with Him!

**"He has never let you down,
never looked the other way when you were being kicked around...
He has been right there, listening."**
Psalm 22:24 (Msg.)

Every promise in the Bible is backed by God and His power. When we pray His promises, we know He hears us and that all the power of Heaven defends His name.

**"When I pray, You answer me
and encourage me by giving me the strength I need."**
Psalm 138:3 (LB)

The Word of God: When I am in the dark, it is light. When I am hungry–it is bread. When I am lost–it is my guide.

"The words I have spoken to you are spirit and they are life."
John 6:63 (NIV)

The Bible is "soul food". Without daily nourishment, we will starve.

**"In the beginning was the Word,
and the Word was with God,
and the Word was God."**
John 1:1 (NAS)

"He spoke a Book and lives in His spoken words...causing the power of them to persist across the years." 5

"...my cry brings me right into His presence–a private audience!"
Psalm 18:6 (Msg.)

From there we can rise to unlimited heights!

**"This is the confidence we have in approaching God:
that if we ask anything according to His Will, He hears us."**
I John 5:14 (NIV)

The Will of God is the same for all. He has no favorites within His household. All He has ever done for any of His children, He will do for all of His children.

**"Pray like this: Our Father in heaven,
may Your name be honored...may Your will be done ..."**
Matthew 6:9, 10 (NLT)

Nothing that is not part of God's will is allowed to come into the life of one of God's children.

**"...call upon Me and come and pray to me,
and I will listen to you."**
Jeremiah 29:12 (NIV)

**"Then those who feared the LORD talked with each other,
and the LORD listened and heard.
A scroll of remembrance was written in His presence**

concerning those who feared him and honored His name."
Malachi 3:16 (NIV)

Spiritual eavesdropping! The Lord listens when His children talk about Him! He even keeps a record!

**"And the Holy Spirit helps us in our distress,
for we don't even know what we should pray for, nor how we should pray.
But the Holy Spirit prays for us with groanings that cannot be expressed in words.
And the Father who knows all hearts knows what the Spirit is saying,
for the Spirit pleads for us believers in harmony with God's own will."**
Romans 8:26, 27 (NLT)

The Lord not only listens and answers our prayers, He helps us pray!

Thoughts

Chapter 3

"The Lord will work out His plans for my life...." Psalm 138:8a (NLT)

In April of 2001, I had another attack. I had severe pain in my head for three months that never went away. The pain caused headaches, but actually, I could feel the pain just by touching my head. It was like my brain was pushing against my skull. I went to my family doctor and she gave me creams and pills and sympathy and wondered looks, but nothing helped. I went back to the neurologist at Barrows. Since he knew I had had an incident previously and now I was having another, he began to think MS. He ordered an MRI which showed lesions on my brain. He gave me a spinal tap which showed the antibodies present that were consistent with MS. He broke the news to me in June 2001. I have never been the same, physically, emotionally, spiritually…arguably, for the better.

It was actually kind of a relief to know the reason for my problems, but on the other hand, MS isn't exactly what I would call a relief. I was shocked and scared and angry and confused. I didn't even really know what MS was, but I knew it had to be bad since the name sounded bad. MULTIPLE SCLEROSIS. I thought I was doomed. I thought my life was over. I wondered how this could happen to me? I am 34 years old! I am a Christian! God promised to love me! I am supposed to be in the prime of my life. I have children to take care of. I have a good job. "Oh God, what is happening to me?"

I started taking an immune-modulating drug for MS. I had to inject myself with a needle daily. God gave me relief from the head pain and I continued working and praising God for His presence in my life. **"He tends His flock like a shepherd. He gathers the lambs in His arms and carries them close to His heart."** Isaiah 40:11a (NIV).

Journal Entry: July 9, 2001. So much has happened, I don't know where to begin. First, I began experiencing headaches that would not go away. I actually had an area on my head that hurt to the touch. It would send shooting pains through my head. Then it grew into a constant dull aching pain in my head. Constant! Every day, all day. It got so bad, I went to the emergency room. They did a CAT scan which showed abnormalities. So then I had an MRI of my brain which showed evidence of multiple sclerosis! I had to start injection therapy! So far, it's awful. One time I injected myself into the muscle and it hurt really bad. I am still trying to ingest all this. I can't believe this is happening. The kids are taking it well, but I'm sure they don't totally grasp it. I still look and act "normal" so they are not too concerned at this point. Heather helps me with my shot sometimes and she gives me an ice pop to put on my skin to ease the pain.

I wrote about an incident in my journal about a year ago describing a time when I had double vision and dizziness and balance problems and motor skills problems, etc. That was an MS attack!!

After I was diagnosed, I found out that my right eye was damaged due to optic neuritis from the last attack. I found out why all those awful things happened to me last year. I found out why I continue to have vision problems in the heat, and the best part...I found out it wasn't just STRESS AND ANXIETY. I have a disease!

I have and am continuing to draw closer to God through all of this. Ken has been supportive. My job has been supportive. Church has been supportive. I still have so much to be thankful for. So why am I so scared?

Devotion

I Have a Plan for Your Life

**"'For I know the plans I have for you', declares the Lord.
'Plans to prosper you and not to harm you.
Plans to give you hope and a future.'"**
Jeremiah 29:11 (NIV)

Our lives have profound meaning! God is very concerned about the direction of our lives. That is why His Word was written!

**"You will keep on guiding me with Your counsel,
leading me to a glorious destiny."**
Psalm 73:24 (NLT)

There is a reason for everything that happens.

**"It is God who directs the lives of His creatures;
everyone's life is in His power."**
Job 12:10 (TEV)

God was thinking of us long before we ever thought about Him.

**"Trust in the Lord with all your heart;
do not lean on your own understanding.
Seek His Will in all you do, and He will direct your paths."**
Proverbs 3:5, 6 (NLT)

We can pray for direction and watch God make our decisions!

**"You saw me before I was born.
Every day of my life was recorded in your book.
Every moment was laid out before a single day had passed."**
Psalm 139:16 (NLT)

A missionary was involved in a car accident one night and was knocked unconscious and taken to the hospital. The next morning he woke up, saw a nurse, and asked what had happened. The nurse said, "I'm sorry, you had an accident." The missionary had a puzzled look on his face when he replied, "Accident? There are no accidents in the life of a Christian, only incidents in God's plan!"

"God charts the road you take." Psalm 1:6a (Msg.)

The Bible exhorts us to be patient and allow the Lord to work in our lives. **"Friends, when life gets really difficult, don't jump to the conclusion that God isn't on the job. Instead, be glad that you**

are in the very thick of what Christ experienced. This is a spiritual refining process, with glory just around the corner." 1 Peter 4:12-13 (Msg.)

Sometimes, it's when things are the most out of control, when God is working the most.

**"In Your unfailing love,
You will lead the people You have redeemed.
In Your strength You will guide them to Your holy dwelling."**
Exodus 15:13 (NIV)

"Without God, life has no purpose, and without purpose, life has no meaning. Without meaning, life has no significance or hope." 6

**"The Lord says,
'I will guide you along the best pathway for your life.
I will advise you and watch over you.'"**
Psalm 32:8 (NLT)

"At first we want the consciousness of being guided by God, then as we go on, we live so much in the consciousness of God that we do not need to ask what His will is, because the thought of choosing any other will never occur to us." 7

**"A man's steps are directed by the Lord.
How then can anyone understand his own way?"**
Proverbs 20:24 (NIV)

Trusting God completely means having faith that He knows what is best for our lives.

**"You chart the path ahead of me and tell me where to stop and rest.
Every moment You know where I am."**
Psalm 139:3 (NLT)

God is actively involved in our lives! Nothing or nobody escapes His notice!

"And the Lord is the One who goes ahead of you..."
Deuteronomy 31:8a (NAS)

God knows our lives from beginning to end!

**"Whether you turn to the right or to the left,
your ears will hear a voice behind you,
saying, 'This is the way; walk in it.'"**
Isaiah 30:21 (NIV)

"Put Jesus Christ in the driver's seat of your life and take your hands off the steering wheel...nothing under His control can ever be out of control." 8

**"For this God is our God forever and ever;
He will be our guide even to the end."**
Psalm 48:14 (NIV)

Sometimes we have our noses in the map all the time and forget to look up and see the view. Enjoy the trip, there's joy in the journey!

**"The steps of the godly are directed by the Lord.
He delights in every detail of their lives."**
Psalm 37:23 (NLT)

The Lord delights in us!

**"From eternity to eternity, I am God.
No one can oppose what I do.
No one can reverse my actions."**
Isaiah 43:13 (NLT)

**"O Lord my God, you have done many miracles for us.
Your plans for us are too numerous to list.
If I tried to recite all your wonderful deeds,
I would never come to the end of them."**
Psalm 40:5 (NLT)

Thoughts

Chapter 4

**"In everything you do,
I want you to be free from the concerns of this life."**
I Corinthians 7:32a (NLT)

Well, Phoenix summers and MS do not mix. I felt like the witch in the Wizard of Oz when she melted into the ground. My vision would go haywire and my energy left me to the point that I did not have the strength to lift my legs in order to walk. God forbid the A/C to ever go out in the car or in the house. This just wasn't going to work. I didn't want to leave my job, my church, my life–but MS was changing everything. I could no longer function properly at work. I was exhausted just walking from the copy room back to my desk. I was forgetting things and not processing my thoughts as I used to, which is a critical requirement when working in a law office. Deadlines, sending lawyers out of state, preparing for trials. I needed my brain.

I was shielding my eyes as if I was in the sun, but I was inside the office at my desk trying to see through double vision. That attracted a few stares and looks of heartbreak and concern from everyone, which is all they knew to do. What are you supposed to do? I didn't even know what I wanted them to say, but no matter what it was, it wasn't the right thing. I don't why. I guess because nobody understood.

I think the worst thing to say for me was: "Oh, I know, I don't feel good either". Okaaayyy, do you mean you have an incurable debilitating disease not-feel-good day or you stayed-up-too-late-last-night day? This may sound harsh but I guess you would have to have MS to understand. I just felt so "not-right" all the time and nobody could see it or feel it except for me. You just don't get MS until you get MS.

Anyway, eventually, I knew I had to leave. It was just too hot and I was just too miserable. Living in the hottest state in the country, in the middle of the desert, and not being able to function in the heat, left me few choices. The life I had planned on and worked so hard for was slipping away. I was so scared and worried. Everything was changing. I was quitting my job! There is such a finality in that. What if I didn't like it there? What if things didn't work out? What if I was making the wrong choice? What if I run out of money? Oh my goodness, Rachel, stop it. I would not even be considering this if God did not cause me to consider it! He is directing my life and even if I don't understand everything, that needs to be okay. I am walking with God, so that means He must be leading me. I know He doesn't want His kids to worry, so I just needed to rest my mind and my soul, and let God makes the decisions.

As it turned out, I left everything. I quit my job, left my church, my home, and my friend and family and I moved across the country to Upper Michigan. Cold, cold, cold, but for me, it was better than HOT.

Journal Entry: June, 2002: I had an awesome incident about three nights ago. The Lord spoke to me. He told me to trust Him. I began to get excited because I was enjoying the fact that He has these plans for me and I was so much at peace. I kept asking Him what His plans were. Of course, He won't tell me everything in advance, but I knew that He was working in my life and good things will happen and I am going to be okay. It was so real. I feel like I am now in close communication with God and that He is with me every step of the way and that I am walking in His will. He is awesome and I feel His hand in my life and I love it. I fall in love with Him over and over again every day. I can't wait to read His Word tomorrow. He is my best friend.

Devotion

Please Don't Worry

"Casting the whole of your care
[all your anxieties, all your worries, all your concerns, once and for all]
on Him, for He cares for you affectionately
and cares about you watchfully."
1 Peter 5:7 (Amp)

The Lord is willing to carry our anxieties and worries, if you let Him.

"You can be sure that God will take care of everything you need..."
Philippians 4:19a (Msg.)

Today is the tomorrow you worried about yesterday!

"So don't worry at all about having enough food and clothing...
your heavenly Father already knows perfectly well that you need them,
and He will give them to you if you give Him first place in your life
and live as He wants you to."
Matthew 6:31-33 (LB)

The Lord wants us to know He hears our cries, He knows our needs and He will not fail us. We are His children and He will never forsake us.

"Be still, and know that I am God."
Psalm 46:10 (NIV)

God is so big, He doesn't have to go anywhere!

"So here's what I want you to do, God helping you:
Take your everyday, ordinary life — your sleeping, eating, going-to-work,
and walking-around life and place it before God as an offering.
Embracing what God does for you is the best thing you can do for Him."
Romans 12:1 (Msg.)

"A weary Christian was lying awake one night trying to hold the world together by his worrying. Then he heard the Lord gently say to him, "Now you go to sleep, Brian, I'll sit up."" 9

"...for I know every thought that comes into your minds."
Ezekiel 11:5b (NLT)

God knows the answers to our problems before we know there is a problem!

> **"Don't worry about anything, instead, pray about everything.
> Tell God what you need, and thank Him for all He has done.
> If you do this, you will experience God's peace,
> which is far more wonderful than the human mind can understand."**
> Philippians 4:6, 7 (NLT)

The Message translates this verse this way: **"Don't fret or worry. Instead of worrying, pray. Let petitions and praises shape your worries into prayers, letting God know your concerns. Before you know it, a sense of God's wholeness, everything coming together for good, will come and settle you down. It's wonderful what happens when Christ displaces worry at the center of your life."**

"God never encounters a problem, never faces a difficulty and has never known defeat. He can open up a way where there is no way–even if it means parting a sea! Be confident that God will deliver you–even though you can't figure out how. Live by faith and let God be God!" 10

> **"And why worry about your clothes?
> Look at the lilies and how they grow.
> They don't work or make their clothing,
> yet Solomon in all his glory
> was not dressed as beautifully as they are.
> And if God cares so wonderfully for flowers
> that are here today and gone tomorrow,
> won't he more surely care for you?
> You have so little faith!"**
> Matthew 6:28-30 (NLT)

The Bible tells us that we can spare ourselves a whole lot of stress and honor God a lot more by turning our problems into prayers.

Even in the midst of his pain and loss, Job trusted his life and future to God:
> **"Nevertheless, His mind concerning me remains unchanged,
> and who can turn Him from His purposes?
> Whatever He wants to do, He does.
> So He will do for me all He has planned..."**
> Job 23:13, 14 (LB)

God controls our destiny!

> **"But I have stilled and quieted myself,
> just as a small child is quiet with its mother.
> Yes, like a small child is my soul within me."**
> Psalm 131:2 (NLT)

"No one can calm the heart like Jesus. Our souls can be quieted as we rest against the Lord and hear His heart beat in the Word." 11

"I am your Creator.

You were in my care even before you were born."
Isaiah 44:2a (CEV)

"Several years ago, USA Today published the results of a poll that asked adults to look back over their lives and share what they most regret wasting time on. Topping the list, 67% of those questioned responded that they regretted they had spent time "worrying."" 12

David says, **"Don't give in to worry or anger;
it only leads to trouble."**
Psalm 37:8 (TEV)

When we become worried or upset, we can come to Him to find comfort and rest.

"...Your Father knows exactly what you need even before you ask him!"
Matthew 6:8b (NLT)

Everything in the world is revolving around God's plan and we are at the center of God's plan!

**"Therefore, do not be anxious for tomorrow;
for tomorrow will care for itself..."**
Matthew 6:34 (NAS)

God is big enough to handle our cares. He's much more experienced at solving problems than we are.

"...for those who honor Him will have all they need."
Psalm 34:9b (NLT)

Most of the things we spend so much time worrying about never happen.

**"So I tell you, don't worry about everyday life —
whether you have enough food, drink, and clothes.
Doesn't life consist of more than food and clothing?
Look at the birds.
They don't need to plant or harvest or put food in barns
because your heavenly Father feeds them.
And you are far more valuable to Him than they are."**
Matthew 6:25, 26 (NLT)

If the natural world around us isn't worrying, neither should the children of God!

"...You give them their food as they need it."
Psalm 145:15b (NLT)

Worry spends today by borrowing trouble.

**"Peace I leave with you, My peace I give you.
I do not give to you as the world gives.**

Do not let your hearts be troubled and do not be afraid."
John 14:27 (NIV)

"There are times when our peace is based upon ignorance, but when we awaken to the facts of life, inner peace is impossible unless it is received from Jesus. When Our Lord speaks peace, He makes peace...it is a peace which comes from looking into His face and realizing His undisturbedness." 13

**"Whatever I have, wherever I am,
I can make it through anything
in the One who makes me who I am."**
Philippians 4:13 (Msg.)

Thoughts

Chapter 5

"For the Lord hears the cries of His needy ones..."
Psalm 69:33 (LB)

My husband's family is from Upper Michigan so that is where we went. After the Paralegal degree and the "moving on up" thing, everything was now in the past.

I was now a stay-at-home wife and mom. Everything is going to be fine, right? My life still means something, right? So why does my life seem empty? Why all of a sudden does it feel like my life is over? Was my mission in life done? I was 35 years old and I asked God, "Is this it? Am I all done?" Oh God, please fill my life, give me a purpose. I don't want to be done!

Well, God filled my life. I had things to do every day–family stuff, church stuff, house stuff. I was content. I did what I could and did no more. I was happy. God had answered my prayers. I no longer needed a job to feel fulfilled. I was beginning to see a different way of life, life at home, life with no deadlines or appointments. It takes time to get used to it, but life does go on. It really does.

God had everything under control. He allowed me to stay home when my kids needed me the most (their teenage years) when they are pushing the envelope at every turn. He gave me the ability to keep the house clean and the meals cooked, something I could not have done while working full-time, and He showed me the life He had planned for me–different than the life I had planned for me, but you know what? It was better. I felt even _more_ fulfilled. I raised my kids. I volunteered my time when I could. I even started an MS Support Group in town. Also, I was able to write this book. **"In His unfailing love, my God will come and help me."** Psalm 59:10a (NLT)

After being in Michigan only a few months, I had another attack. My first thought was, "Oh, God, rescue me again, please". **"In my distress, I cried out to the Lord; yes, I prayed to my God for help. He heard me from His sanctuary; my cry reached His ears."** Psalm 18:6 (NLT)

The attack lasted for five months. I got IV steroids from the hospital for three days and then took Prednisone for a couple of weeks. I was so dizzy, I could not see straight. I had numbness on the entire left side of my body, from the bottom of my feet to the top of my head. I stumbled around until I learned how to fall into walls to keep from falling to the ground. I found out if you learn to stumble, it is easier to get around. It becomes just the way things are.

The family pitched in to help me around the house and I clung to my Lord until the storm passed once again. God did restore me and more importantly, He restored my soul. What a joy to see the hand of God in my life! I let the picture of His love overshadow all my problems and now, when I look back on them, I see His miracles in my life more clearly than I see the hardships. I have become thankful for such sweet memories. **"Just as the mountains surround and protect Jerusalem, so the Lord surrounds and protects His people, both now and forever."** Psalm 125:2 (NLT). How blessed are the children of God! I wanted my response to glorify God by allowing my faith to grow stronger as a result of His provision for me. I was learning how to show God that I could praise Him IN the storm, and not just AFTER it. I know that all things have a purpose and I know His purposes for me are good and they cause me to grow closer to Him.

Journal Entry: August 13, 2002: I am in Michigan. I am not in Arizona. It was just a few months ago but already my memories of that life are growing dim. (MS clouds the mind.) Thank you, Lord for giving me the courage, the means, and the strength, to leave everything behind. You are wonderful and awesome—so loving and caring and perfect in all Your ways. On a different note, I believe I am suffering with an MS attack. I have been for a couple of weeks. My balance is way off, my equilibrium is off, not able to get coordinated. It's hard to walk in the straight line and my legs are weak. The only bathroom is upstairs and I have found myself crawling up them...

Devotion

I Will Help You

"The Lord is close to the brokenhearted;
He rescues those who are crushed in spirit."
Psalm 34:18

Before we can understand suffering, we must first understand God's love.

"You keep track of all my sorrows.
You have collected all my tears in Your bottle.
You have recorded each one in Your book."
Psalm 56:8 (NLT)

God is not blind. He sees our sorrows and already has plans to work everything for our good in a way that we cannot even comprehend.

"The Lord nurses them when they are sick
and eases their pain and discomfort."
Psalm 41:3 (NLT)

When we're sick we have a special caregiver, the Lord Himself!

"The Lord helps the fallen
and lifts up those bent beneath their loads."
Psalm 145:14 (NLT)

Worn out? We can come to Jesus with the things that are weighing us down and let Him lift them from our shoulders. We aren't built to carry them ourselves.

"Pile your troubles on God's shoulders–He'll carry your load, He'll help you out."
Psalm 55:22 (Msg.)

"My help comes from the Lord,
Who made the heavens and the earth!
He will not let you stumble and fall;
the One Who watches over you will not sleep."
Psalm 121:2,3 (NLT)

God stays up so we don't have to.

> "I created you and have cared for you since before you were born.
> I will be your God throughout your lifetime–until your hair is white with age.
> I made you and I will care for you. I will carry you along and be your Savior."
> Isaiah 46:3b, 4 (LB)

When we don't understand God's ways, we have to trust Him.

> "Commit everything you do to the Lord.
> Trust Him and He will help you."
> Psalm 37:5 (NLT)

Focus on God's power to deliver rather than the enemy's power to destroy.

> "The Lord hears His people when they call to Him for help.
> He rescues them from all their troubles."
> Psalm 34:17 (NLT)

The more we read the Word, the more our faith in God will grow.

> "The Lord is my shepherd. I have everything I need."
> Psalm 23:1 (NLT)

> "Though they stumble, they will not fall,
> for the Lord holds them by the hand."
> Psalm 37:24 (NLT)

Picture a child holding on to Daddy's hand!

> "For I am the Lord your God Who holds your right hand,
> and Who says to you, 'Do not be afraid. I will help you'."
> Isaiah 41:13 (NIV)

Earth has no trouble that our Lord cannot handle.

> "I waited patiently for the Lord to help me,
> and He turned to me and heard my cry.
> He lifted me out of the pit of despair...
> He set my feet on solid ground and steadied me as I walked along.
> He has given me a new song to sing, a hymn of praise to our God.
> Many will see what He has done and be astounded.
> They will put their trust in the Lord."
> Psalm 40:1-3 (NLT)

God's timing is perfect and His ways are higher than we could imagine. He reminds us,
**"For just as the heavens are higher than the earth,
so are My ways higher than your ways
and My thoughts higher than your thoughts."**
Isaiah 55:9 (Amp)

"In His unfailing love, my God will come and help me."
Psalm 59:10a (NLT)

When we take Him at His word, our hearts are at peace.

**"Wait for the Lord;
be strong and take heart and wait for the Lord."**
Psalm 27:14 (NIV)

When we wait quietly for the Lord to help us, we will not be shaken by the troubles that come into our lives.

**"I wait quietly before God...
He alone is my rock and my salvation,
my fortress where I will never be shaken."**
Psalm 62:1, 2 (NLT)

The NKJV version translates verse 2b, "... I shall not be greatly moved."

When we're settled in the Lord, the movement is only on the surface, not in the depths of our soul.

"And God said...And it was so..."
Genesis 1:9 (NIV)

Our natural reaction is usually some kind of anxiety, but the Lord wants to train us to immediately pass the problem to Him.

**"So let us come boldly to the throne of our gracious God.
There we will receive His mercy,
and we will find grace to help us when we need it."**
Hebrews 4:16 (NLT)

God does not ask us to figure it out, He only asks us to BELIEVE.

**"I took my troubles to the Lord,
I cried out to Him, and He answered my prayer."**
Psalm 120:1 (NLT)

The first thing to remember when we face a problem is that the Lord wants to help us.

**"O Lord my God,
I cried out to You for help,
and You restored my health."**
Psalm 30:2 (NLT)

Times of sickness are opportunities to see the grace of God at work in our lives.

**"He heals the brokenhearted, binding up their wounds...
His understanding is beyond comprehension."**
Psalm 147:3, 5b (NLT)

Those who come to the Lord with broken hearts will not leave with broken hearts.

**"Come and see what our God has done,
what awesome miracles He does for His people!"**
Psalm 66:5 (NLT)

Thoughts

Chapter 6

"...The Lord is my helper, so I will not be afraid..."
Hebrews 13:6b (NLT)

I applied for Social Security Disability and my husband worked very hard to supply for the family. We could have never survived in Phoenix with the high cost of living there, with me not working. God wanted us in Michigan because He knew we could wait on Him in this small town where housing was cheap and life was slow. We waited on God to work in our lives. We had left everything and felt like we were starting out again like we were just married.

After one year, I was approved for Social Security Disability. Thank you, Lord. We bought a one-story house (no stairs), Ken was working, and the kids were enjoying school. Life was beginning to look normal again. **"I love the Lord because He hears my prayers. Because He bends down and listens, I will pray as long as I have breath!"** Psalm 116:1,2 (NLT). MS had gotten a hold of us, but it didn't get a hold of God.

God was taking such good care of us. My children are older now and able to wash their own clothes, make some of their own meals, and help around the house. When I have an attack, my daughter cooks and cleans and my son takes care of the yard and garbage. My husband is very supportive and does what I cannot do. I am so thankful.

I believed that I needed to get my affairs in order before it was time for me to attend to my affairs in heaven. The most important affair in my life was to grow stronger in faith and be refined by God's hand.

I walked hand in hand with my heavenly Father all day long. We shared everything with each other. I was at a place in my life spiritually that I had never been before. I felt so close to God, I had no fear of the future. It was through my weaknesses that I felt His strength and I was confident that, with His strength, I could make it through anything. I had more joy in my soul after I was diagnosed with MS than I ever had before I was diagnosed. The unexplainable became the understandable.

"I prayed to the Lord, and He answered me, freeing me from all my fears." Psalm 34:4 (NLT)

Journal Entry: December 5, 2004: ...I learned something new today. The Bible talks about not worshiping idols and the usual thing I think of is, of course, money, things, people, etc. But what hadn't occurred to me was that good things can be idols–such as having a good, pain-free life or even happiness. If that is my first goal, it is an idol. When something is so important to me that I would sin to get it or sin when I don't get it, it is an idol. My focus on all things has to be glorifying God. That is when joy transcends happiness. Joy is on a completely different level. Thank you, Lord, for continuing to speak to me through Your Word. I continue to learn new things from the same words I have read over and over again and it will continue to be that way forevermore. I praise Your Holy name for all my living days...

Devotion

I Don't Want You to be Afraid

**"Do not fear, for I am with you,
Do not anxiously look about you,
For I am your God.
I will strengthen you, surely I will help you.
Surely, I will uphold you with My righteous right hand."**
Isaiah 41:10 (NASB)

**"I prayed to the Lord and He answered me,
freeing me from all my fears."**
Psalm 34:4 (NLT)

Lots of people struggle with fear. If we were all alone in this world, we should be afraid, but we're not. We are children of the Almighty God.

**"The Lord is with me; I will not be afraid…
The Lord is with me;
He is my Helper."**
Psalm 118:6,7a (NIV)

God often comforts us, not necessarily by changing our circumstances, but by calming our fears toward them.

**"I cried out to the Lord in my suffering, and He heard me.
He set me free from all my fears."**
Psalm 34:6 (NLT)

"The remarkable thing about fearing God, is that when you fear God, you fear nothing else, whereas, if you do not fear God, you fear everything else." [14]

**"Don't fear anything except the Lord of the armies of heaven!
If you fear Him, you need fear nothing else."**
Isaiah 8:13 (LB)

Let me not pray to be sheltered from dangers, but to be fearless in facing them.

**"I, even I, am He Who comforts you.
Who are you that you fear mortal men,
The sons of men, who are but grass,
that you forget the Lord your Maker,
Who stretched out the heavens
and laid the foundations of the earth…**

**For I am the Lord your God,
Who churns up the sea so that its waves roar--
The Lord Almighty is His Name!"**
Isaiah 51:12,13a,15 (NIV)

The antidote for fear is knowing God's love.

"But when I am afraid, I put my trust in You."
Psalm 56:3 (NLT)

"Be my feelings what they will, Jesus is my Savior still!" 15

It helps to remember what the Lord has done for us in the past.
**"I recall all You have done, O Lord;
I remember Your wonderful deeds of long ago.
They are constantly in my thoughts.
I cannot stop thinking about them."**
Psalm 77:11,12 (NLT)

"The wise man in the storm prays to God, not for safety from danger, but for deliverance from fear. It is the storm within which endangers him, not the storm without." 16

**"Praise be to the God and Father of our Lord Jesus Christ,
the Father of compassion and the God of all comfort,
Who comforts us in all our troubles..."**
2 Corinthians 1:3,4a (NIV)

"In the midst of the awfulness, a touch comes, and you know it is the right hand of Jesus Christ...once His touch comes, nothing at all can cast you into fear again." 17

**"Be strong and courageous.
Do not be afraid or discouraged...
for there is greater power within us than with him.
With him is only the arm of flesh, but with us is
the Lord our God to help us
and to fight our battles."**
2 Chronicles 32:78a (NIV)

"Fear came knocking at the door, faith answered, and no one was there." 18

"Do not tremble, do not be afraid."
Isaiah 44:8 (NIV)

The measure of your comfort will always be the measure of your confidence in God.

> **"I can lay down and sleep in safety,
> for the Lord is watching over me."**
> Psalm 3:5

God never gets tired! He has perfect power all the time.

> **"I will lie down in peace and sleep,
> for You alone, O Lord, will keep me safe."**
> Psalm 4:8 (NLT)

Whenever God allows extraordinary trials, He gives extraordinary comfort.

> **"You can lie down without fear and enjoy pleasant dreams…
> for the Lord is your security."**
> Proverbs 3:24,26a (NLT)

> **"The Lord is the everlasting God,
> the Creator of the ends of the earth.
> He will not grow tired or weary,
> and His Understanding, no one can fathom.
> He gives strength to the weary,
> and increases the power of the weak…
> those who hope in the Lord will renew their strength.
> They will soar on wings like eagles,
> they will run and not grow weary,
> they will walk and not be faint."**
> Isaiah 40:28b,29,31 (NIV)

Times of hardship and trial can make us feel lonely and vulnerable, but God is with us whether we can see Him or not. He's with us regardless of how we feel.

> **"You came near when I called You, and You said, 'Do not fear"."**
> Lamentations 3:57 (NIV)

"People are like tea bags – you have to put them in hot water before you know how strong they are." [19]

> **"Do not be fainthearted.
> Do not be afraid, or panic or tremble before them,
> for the Lord your God in the One who goes with you,
> to fight for you against your enemies, to save you."**
> Deuteronomy 20:3b,4 (NASB)

The cure for fear is faith in God and in His Word and a realization that today and every day, Jesus is always right beside us. We are not on our own!

"Do not be afraid, for I am with you." Isaiah 43:5 (NIV)

Every need we have provides God with the opportunity to show us His love and power.

"…with Him on my side, I'm fearless, afraid of no one and nothing"
Psalm 27:1 (Msg.)

Dark days don't last forever. That is when we need to turn on the light of God's Word.

**"God can do anything you know –
far more than you could ever imagine or guess or request in your wildest dreams.**
Ephesians 3:20 (Msg.)

Thoughts

Chapter 7

"...when I needed You, You were there..."
Psalm 9:4 (Msg.)

I started to home school my daughter when she was in high school because I felt she needed teaching about God's Word, something she would never get in public school. Unfortunately though, after one semester, I had an attack and I could not talk properly. My words were slurred. I sounded as if I were drunk. So, I had to send her back to school.

Back to the hospital for IV treatments, and as bad as steroids are for us, they do help get rid of the short term effects of these attacks, and they work very quickly. I was back to almost normal in a couple of weeks. **"...In the secret place of His tent, He will hide me..."** Psalm 27:5 (NAS).

God directs my steps. He wanted me to fill my daughter's life with what He wanted her to have and when He was done, He sent her back to school. It had nothing to do with me. It had everything to do with Him. **"You will keep on guiding me with Your counsel, leading me to a glorious destiny."** Psalm 73:24 (NLT).

Ken and the kids are always very understanding and very supportive. They help me when I need help and they have learned to pull together and run the household when I can't do it. It is just another blessing in my life to see the love of my family for me, especially from teenagers, whose worlds usually only revolve around themselves.

I had another attack in March, 2005, my 5th. I was extremely dizzy and I had severe double vision. I could not watch TV, and of course, I couldn't read and I couldn't drive. It was even difficult to walk. My head felt like it was in the clouds. I wasn't seeing reality as normal. I couldn't think clearly, and therefore, I couldn't pray as well as I wanted. I asked the Holy Spirit to pray for me.

It was months before I began to feel okay again. It's as if the world stops and I am clueless to what's going on around me. When I began to start seeing more clearly, I was able to think more clearly. I was getting better. The attacks are not like they used to be though, my soul is at peace now and I am more acutely aware that God is right by my side every minute of the day.

"My soul holds on to you. Your right hand holds me up." Psalm 63:8

Journal Entry: March 29, 2005: ...I have been sick with an MS attack...but what I really want to say is this–I have handled this trial like no other. I have not lost my joy in my heavenly Daddy and I am completely at peace with what is happening. I know that all things have a purpose and I want to grow and mature from it. God is so faithful. I will not doubt or waver or be angry or sad or scared or depressed–those are ungodly responses. I have been purchased with a high price–my life is not my own. I will make it through this and then I will give glory to God, for my joy is in Him...

Devotion

I Will Stay Right by Your Side

"...I am with you, declares the Lord Almighty."
Haggai 2:4 (NIV)

We have the Promise of His Presence!

Because we are so special to God, He will hide us **"in His sanctuary"**. Psalm 27:5 (NLT), **"in the shelter of His presence"** Psalm 31:20 (NIV). God keeps us so close to Him that we are always in His shadow!

**"He tends His flock like a shepherd.
He gathers the lambs in His arms and carries them close to His heart."**
Isaiah 40:11a (NIV)

Listen carefully today to hear the heartbeat of His love.

"My soul holds on to you. Your right hand holds me up."
Psalm 63:8 (NLV)

"God has said, 'I will never leave you or let you be alone.'"
Hebrews 13:5b (NLV)

The Amplified Version translates this verse this way: **"...I will not in any way fail you nor give you up nor leave you without support. [I will] not, [I will] not, [I will] not in any degree leave you helpless, nor forsake nor let [you] down, [relax My hold on you]. —Assuredly not!"**

Jesus knows what it's like to be deserted. The experience of being "left" or "deserted" happened repeatedly in His ministry. At one point in His ministry the Bible says that **"At this point, many of His disciples turned away and deserted him."** (John 6:66). Therefore, His words take on special meaning when He says: **"...I will be with you; I will not fail you or forsake you."** Joshua 1:5b (NAS) 20
"The knowledge that we are never alone calms the troubled sea of our lives and speaks peace to our souls." 21

His glory surrounds you in the spiritual realm–**"For I, declares the Lord, will be a wall of fire around her, and I will be the glory in her midst."** Zechariah 2:5 (NAS)

"God is everywhere, close to everything, next to everyone." 22

**"I know the Lord is always with me.
I will not be shaken; for He is right beside me."**
Psalm 16:8 (NLT)

"...In the secret place of His tent, He will hide me..."
Psalm 27:5 (NAS)

Hang on to your song by staying close to the composer.

"I can never escape from Your spirit! I can never get away from Your presence! If I go up to heaven, You are there; if I go down to the place of the dead, You are there. If I ride the wings of the morning, if I dwell by the farthest oceans, even there Your hand will guide me, and Your strength will support me. I could ask the darkness to hide me and the light around me to become night — but even in darkness I cannot hide from You. To You the night shines as bright as day. Darkness and light are both alike to you." Psalm 139:7-12 (NLT)

As long as God is in our boat during the storm, we will not drown.

**"Even if my father and mother abandon me,
the Lord will hold me close."**
Psalm 27:10 (NLT)

Our Daddy in heaven is the closest family we will ever have.

"I will hide beneath the shadow of your wings until this violent storm is past."
Psalm 57:1b (NLT)

The Lord wants us to know that He will walk through it with us.

**"The Lord is watching everywhere,
keeping His eye on both the evil and the good."**
Proverbs 15:3 (NLT)

"Nothing in all creation can hide from Him."
Hebrews 4:13 (NLT)

"No one, in mere distance, is any further from or any nearer to God than any other person." 23

**"I am everywhere—both near and far, in heaven and on earth.
There are no secret places where you can hide from me."**
Jeremiah 23:23, 24 (CEV)

Jesus gives us the encouragement of His presence. **"I'll be with you, day after day after day, right up to the end of the age."** Matthew 28:20 (Msg.)

"A spiritual kingdom lies among us, enclosing us, embracing us, altogether within reach of our inner selves, waiting for us to recognize it. God Himself is here waiting our response to His presence." 24

"And so I walk in the Lord's presence as I live here on earth."
Psalm 116:9 (NLT)

Thoughts

Chapter 8

"God is our refuge and strength, always ready to help in times of trouble. So we will not fear, even if earthquakes come and the mountains crumbled into the sea."
Psalm 46:1 2 (NLT)

Well, you guessed it. I am having another attack. Number 6. February, 2006. It was, I believe, the worst attack I have ever had. It has been 7 years since my first attack, so I imagine the disease is progressing. My doctor told me I was suffering with autonomic system failure – the system which controls all of our involuntary bodily functions that we take for granted, such as digestion, heartbeat, body temperature, blood pressure, swallowing, organ function, blinking, etc. The peripheral nerves involved in these processes were malfunctioning and even shutting down.

I could not sit upright for longer than a few seconds, not even just slightly elevated with a pillow. I had to be flat on my back or be extremely ill. My heart was pounding/racing, I was cold and then hot and then cold again. My hands felt like they had frostbite, I was wearing gloves inside the house to keep them warm. My feet were freezing so badly, they burned, to the point that it was intolerable. I tried to soak them and wrap them with cold cloths, rub them with creams, take pain pills–nothing worked. My ears were ringing very loudly and I was so dizzy, and sleeping didn't help, it only made me nauseous. One week I had diarrhea and the next week, constipated. I had a hard time eating or drinking because of the inability to swallow properly, but even if I could swallow, I couldn't eat a lot at one time because my body could not digest. I lost 6 lbs., even though I was not getting exercise and I was on Prednisone, which usually causes weight gain. My legs were extremely weak and shaky. If I tried to bend down, I would fall. My legs could not hold me up. Even breathing was difficult and exhausting.

Once I was able to sit upright, I was exhausted to the point of extreme illness after just a few minutes. It's hard to explain what I mean by "illness". I guess imagine your worst flu and how you were just melted into the couch and your skin hurt and your body ached and you didn't care about anything going on around you. Multiply that by 10 and you would be close. When the attack was finally easing up to the point that I could walk around the house, I just felt as if someone had hooked a Shop-vac to my chest and sucked out every bit of energy that ever existed within me. Like I was trying to swim but somebody was holding onto my legs. I could sleep 20 hours a day, 7 days a week, and still be exhausted.

The attack felt like it was lasting forever, I was feeling so badly, I just cried out to God, out loud, all day long (my family was gone to work and school), begging for mercy and healing and for Him to rescue me and hear my prayers and the prayers of all those praying for me, and you know what? God reached down and touched me. He rescued me. He heard our prayers. He loved me and had compassion on me and, by that night, I was actually feeling better–for the first time in forever.

I was so amazed and grateful and thankful and I felt so loved and cared for. I will never cease to give God glory and praise and honor and thanks for all the days of my life for the wonderful blessing of showing me that He was there for me when I needed Him the most. That is how I can say that MS has a way of being a blessing in my life. I saw the hand of God and I will never forget it.

"From where He sits, He overlooks all us earth-dwellers...He watches everything we do...the one who are looking for His love. He's ready to come to their rescue in bad times." Psalm 33:15,18 (Msg.)

Journal Entry: April 15, 2006: ...I still haven't recovered completely from the attack. My equilibrium is way off so it's hard to keep my balance. I am weak and shaky still, so needless to say, I don't do much. My right arm and hand are still numb, but my left leg is coming back...it was burning so badly, it made me cry....

Devotion

Trust Me in Times of Trouble

**"Trust Me in your times of trouble,
and I will rescue you, and you will give Me glory."**
Psalm 50:15 (NLT)

Trouble will have one of two affects in our lives. It will either pull us away from the Lord or push us close to Him. It is our choice.

**"You cried to Me in trouble and I saved you;
I answered out of the thundercloud."**
Psalm 81:7a (NLT)

There are four absolutes we can build our lives upon. We need to make up our minds that we will never doubt or question them. Put them on your refrigerator or dashboard or computer:
God is in control. God loves you. God is good. God has a plan. 25

**"I am overcome with joy because of Your unfailing love,
for You have seen my troubles,
and You care about the anguish of my soul."**
Psalm 31:7 (NLT)

"Don't be troubled by trouble. Circumstances cannot change the character of God." 26

"There is no need to fear when times of trouble come..."
Psalm 49:5a (NLT)

**"From where He sits He overlooks all us earth-dwellers...
He watches everything we do...the ones who are looking for His love.
He's ready to come to their rescue in bad times."**
Psalm 33:15, 18 (Msg.)

"Have you ever been tempted to give up? Tempted to lose heart? If you have, you join the company of great men and women of God, like Moses, David, Elijah, Isaiah, Jeremiah, and Paul. Discouragement comes to everyone. That is why God gives us comfort and encouragement in His Word. 27 Let's look...
**"The Lord is good, a refuge in times of trouble. He cares for those who trust in Him."
Nahum 1:7 (NIV)**

Anxiety is caused by looking first at the circumstances and then looking at God. Faith calls for looking first at God and then looking at the circumstance in the light of God's power and God's strength. **"...
fixing our eyes on Jesus, the author and perfector of faith ..."** Hebrews 12:2a (NASB)

One person with God is the Majority!

"...we're not sure what to do, but we know that God knows what to do..."
2 Corinthians 4:7b (Msg.)

God has a purpose behind every problem.

**"All you need to remember is that God will never let you down;
He'll never let you be pushed past your limit;
He'll always be there to help you come through it."**
I Corinthians 10:13b (Msg.)

Our troubles will bring blessings because they are God's chariots of grace.

**"Then Jesus said, 'Come to me, all of you who are weary and carry heavy burdens,
and I will give you rest'."**
Matthew 11:28 (NLT)

All our troubles are seen by the Lord and, because He loves us, He can't see them without doing something about them.

"The Lord delivers me in times of trouble."
Psalm 37:39

Never doubt in the dark what God has shown you in the light.

**"You're blessed when you're at the end of your rope.
With less of you there is more of God...."**
Matthew 5:3 (Msg.)

When God places a burden upon us, He places His arms underneath us.

**"We felt we were doomed to die and saw how powerless we were to help ourselves,
but that was good, for then we put everything into the hands of God,
Who alone could save us..."**
2 Corinthians 1:9 (LB)

"It can be a comforting thought that trouble, in whatever form it comes to us, is a heavenly messenger that brings us something from God." 28

"We live by faith, not by sight." 2 Corinthians 5:7 (NIV). **"Now faith is being sure of what we hope for and certain of what we do not see."** Hebrews 11:1 (NIV). **"...the outcome of your faith is the salvation of your souls."** I Peter 1:9 (NASB)

Faith should not diminish with bad news, it should be strengthened. Faith makes the weak strong.

"...your faith has made you well."
Mark 5:34 (NLT)

"Three men were walking on a wall–Feeling, Faith, and Fact. When Feeling got an awful fall, and Faith was taken back, so close was Faith to Feeling, He stumbled and fell, too. But Fact remained, and pulled Faith back, And Faith brought Feeling, too!" 29

"Because of faith, Christ has brought us into this place of highest privilege..."
Romans 5:2a (NLT)

"Faith honors God, and God honors faith." 30

**"And Abram believed the LORD,
and the LORD declared him righteous because of his faith."**
Genesis 15:6

By Faith, we obtain God's blessings!

**"Blessed are those who endure when they are tested.
When they pass the test, they will receive the crown of life
that God has promised to those who love Him."**
James 1:12 (GWT)

Thoughts

Chapter 9

"The righteous face many troubles, but the Lord rescues them from each and every one. For the Lord protects them from harm..."
Psalm 34:19 (NIV)

Many people with MS look "normal" and therefore, most people have a hard time understanding what a person with MS goes through. They do not understand that there are times of attack and there are times of "dysfunctionally normal" I don't blame them. I would have a hard time understanding too. The reality is, people with MS do not ever feel normal or right or comfortable or healthy, like someone who doesn't have a chronic disease or illness.

It is now 2014, I have had MS for 15 years. I have had 12 attacks. I am still walking, although with a cane. God came up with a fantastic new drug called Tysabri. It has made kept me attack free for over 4 years. This book does not end with a miraculous cure for MS. No, I still have MS. But this book ends with a sick person who is better than then the healthy person I left behind. I have more God, great faith, perseverance, longsuffering, steadfastness, and devotion to the important things in life.

I believe that God gives us a testimony through our experiences in order to help others going through their experiences. God gives us comfort and love so that we may show others comfort and love.

My desire is that you can begin to look at the hardships through God's eyes and see that MS or any other suffering can be a blessing, because it brings us directly into the presence of God's grace and compassion. When I look back on my attacks, I remember God's provision for me in a powerful way, more than the pain.

You must give your life to God Almighty and He will fulfill all the promises written in this book. You will finally see and hear and touch and taste what God's compassion and grace really is!

"But as for me, I will sing about Your power. I will shout with joy each morning because of Your unfailing love. For You have been my refuge, a place of safety in the day of distress. Psalm 59:16 (NLT).

Devotion

I Will Protect You

**"For You are my hiding place; You protect me from trouble.
You surround me with songs of victory."**
Psalm 32:7 (NLT)

Though everything around us may appear to be shaking, Jesus, the Rock on which we stand, never moves!

"See, God has come to save me!"
Isaiah 12:2a (LB)

Our Daddy in heaven will move mountains for you!

**"All you who fear the Lord, trust the Lord!
He is your helper, He is your shield."**
Psalm 115:11 (NLT)

We protect our kids with our limited strength. God protects His kids with His unlimited power!

**"Oh, love the Lord, all of you who are His people;
for the Lord protects those who are loyal to Him...
So, cheer up! Take courage if you are depending on the Lord."**
Psalm 31:23, 24 (LB)

In the first century, a shield-bearer, holding his shield, would go several feet in front of the soldier in order to protect him. Picture Jesus going before you, as your shield, throughout your life!

**"You have done so much for those who come to You for protection,
blessing them before the watching world.
You hide them in the shelter of your presence."**
Psalm 31:19b, 20a (NLT)

Walking in God's presence provides a shelter for us.

**"But as for me, I will sing about Your power.
I will shout with joy each morning because of Your unfailing love.
For You have been my refuge, a place of safety in the day of distress."**
Psalm 59:16 (NLT)

What God has done for you in the past is proof of the promise of His provision in the future.

"...I trust in Your unfailing love, I will rejoice because You have rescued me."
Psalm 13:5 (NLT)

We are loved by God, therefore we can trust Him!

"The Lord says, 'I will rescue those who love Me.
I will protect those who trust in My name.
When they call Me, I will answer;
I will be with them in trouble.
I will rescue them and honor them.'"
Psalm 91:14-16 (NLT)

"Though winds are wild, and the gale unleashed, My trusting heart still sings: I know that they mean no harm to me, He rides upon their wings!" 31

"The Lord will fight for you; you need only to be still."
Exodus 14:14 (NIV)

We must face trouble in order to witness being rescued by God.

"You are my strength; I wait for you to rescue me,
for you, O God, are my place of safety."
Psalm 59:9 (NLT)

What a joy to see the hand of God in your life! Let it overshadow your problems!

"Just as the mountains surround and protect Jerusalem,
so the Lord surrounds and protects His people, both now and forever."
Psalm 125:2 (NLT)

We are surrounded by God's love and protection! We are His children! How blessed are the children of God!

"The Lord is a strong fortress. The godly run to Him and are safe."
Proverbs 18:10 (LB)

Years ago, a national magazine carried the story of a forest fire in Yellowstone National Park. After the fire, forest rangers began their trek up the mountain to assess the inferno's damage. One ranger found a bird literally petrified in the ashes perched like a statue at the base of a tree.
Somewhat sickened by the eerie sight, he knocked over the bird with a stick. When he struck it, three tiny chicks scurried from under their dead mother's wings. The mother, keenly aware of the impending danger, instinctively moved her offspring to the safest place, under her wings.
She could have flown to safety and saved herself, but she refused to abandon her babies. When the inferno arrived she covered the chicks with her wings and bravely held her ground. Her scorched remains were a testimony of her sacrifice. Because she was willing to die, those under the covering of her wings would live. 32

"He will shield you with His wings. He will shelter you with His feathers.

His faithful promises are your armor and protection."
Psalm 91:4 (NLT)

God is our hiding place.

"Jehovah Himself is caring for you! He is your Defender.
He protects you day and night.
He keeps His eye upon you as you come and go, and always guards you."
Psalm 121:5,6,8 (LB)

"There is nothing — no circumstance, no trouble, no testing—that can ever touch me until, first of all, it has gone past God and past Christ, right through to me. If it has come that far, it has come with great purpose, which we may not understand at the moment; but as I refuse to become panicky, as I lift my eyes up to Him and accept it as coming from the Throne of God for some great purpose of blessing, no sorrow will ever disturb me, no trial will ever disarm me, no circumstance will cause me to fret, for I shall rest in the joy of what my Lord is." 33

"The LORD is my strength, my shield from every danger.
I trust in Him with all my heart.
He helps me, and my heart is filled with joy.
I burst out in songs of thanksgiving."
Psalm 28:7 (NLT)

Be assured, if we walk with Him and look to Him and expect help from Him, He will never fail us.

"The Lord is a refuge for the oppressed, a stronghold in times of trouble".
Psalm 9:9 (NIV)

There are times when we suffer a lot and go through hard times. Rather than fighting them, know that God is working through these situations and trust that His way is perfect. **"As for God, His way is perfect. All the Lord's promises prove true. He is a shield for all who look to Him for protection."**
Psalm 18:30 (NLT)

We honor those who rescue others as heroes and give them medals. The Lord is worthy of our honor for rescuing us every day.

A single stroke of lightning, which is usually 3-4 miles long, travels at a speed of up to 100,000 miles per second, or half the speed of light. At that speed, it's impossible to see that the bolt is actually traveling from the ground up to the clouds. But in a single flash, it can carry 100 million volts of electricity and reach a temperature of 55,000 degrees Fahrenheit, 5 times hotter than the surface of the sun! Earth is struck by at least 100 strokes of lightning every second. That's more than 8.6 million strikes a day!

"He fills His hands with lightning bolts. He hurls each at its target."
Job 36:32 (LB)

God is all powerful! He can protect us against any force this world can offer. We can trust Him to take care of our needs.

God also protects us by sending us His holy angels.

**"For He orders His Angels to protect you wherever you go.
They will hold you with their hands..."**
Psalm 91:11, 12a (NLT)

Angels are involved in your life!

**"...Angels are...servants.
They are spirits sent from God to care for those who will receive salvation."**
Hebrews 1:14 (NLT)

God orders angels to protect you wherever you go.

"For the angel of the Lord guards and rescues all who reverence Him."
Psalm 34:7 (LB)

Angels are ready to do spiritual battle for us and against the forces of darkness, at God's command.

**"Praise the Lord, you angels of His,
you mighty creatures who carry out His plans,
listening for each of His commands."**
Psalm 103:20 (NLT)

Angels escort us to Jesus when we die! (Luke 16:22)

"Yes, praise the Lord, you armies of angels, who serve Him and do His Will!"
Psalm 103:21 (NLT)

Some of the most difficult times in my life are the most precious times in my life. Nearness to God can be the answer to all of our anxieties and sufferings. To dwell in God's presence is the glory of living. I would not replace it with all the riches and health in the world.

If you have a handicap of any kind, an illness or any other problem, God CAN use you! He loves you and wants to glorify Himself through your weaknesses. He wants to show the world that you are valuable and you are loved. Remember, our strength comes from God, not from ourselves. **"I am glad to boast about my weaknesses, so that the power of Christ may work through me.** 2 Corinthians 12:9-10a (NLT). Knowing this, I am quite content with my weaknesses.

"And I pray that Christ will be more and more at home in your hearts as you trust in Him. May your roots go down deep into the soil of God's marvelous love, and may you have the power to understand, as all God's people should, how wide, how long, how high, and how deep His love really is. May you experience the love of Christ, though it is so great you will never fully understand it. Then you will be filled with the fullness of life and power that comes from God." Ephesians 3:17-19 (NLT)

"The amazing grace of the Master Jesus Christ, the extravagant love of God, the intimate friendship of the Holy Spirit, be with all of you." 2 Corinthians 13:14 (Msg.)

Thoughts

Endnotes

1. Grace Mail, Pastor J. Martin, Calvary Community Church, Phoenix, Arizona, www.calvaryphx.com

2. Ibid

3. Ibid

4. Grace Mail, Pastor J. Martin, Calvary Community Church, Phoenix, Arizona, www.calvaryphx.com

5. The Pursuit of God , A.W. Tozer , pg. 71

6. A Purpose Driven Life, Rick Warren, pg. 30

7. My Utmost for His Highest, Oswald Chambers, The Secret of the Lord

8. A Purpose Driven Life, Rick Warren, pg. 83

9. Grace Mail, Pastor J. Martin, Calvary Community Church, Phoenix, Arizona, www.calvaryphx.com

10. Ibid

11. Ibid

12. USA Today Snapshots 5/22/00

13. My Utmost for His Highest, Oswald Chambers, Are you ever Disturbed?

14. Oswald Chambers, author of My Utmost for His Highest

15. Grace Mail, Pastor J. Martin, Calvary Community Church, Phoenix, Arizona, www.calvaryphx.com

16. Ralph Waldo Emerson , 17th century American poet

17. My Utmost for His Highest, Oswald Chambers, In Delight of Despair

18. Charles Spurgeon, 17th century British Baptist preacher

19. Grace Mail, Pastor J. Martin, Calvary Community Church, Phoenix, Arizona, www.calvaryphx.com

20. Ibid

21. The Knowledge of the Holy, A.W. Tozer

22. The Knowledge of the Holy, A.W. Tozer, p. 116

23. The Pursuit of God, A.W. Tozer, pg. 58

24. The Pursuit of God, A.W. Tozer, pg. 50

25. Grace Mail, Pastor J. Martin, Calvary Community Church, Phoenix, Arizona, www.calvaryphx.com

26. A Purpose Driven Life, Rick Warren, pg. 111

27. Grace Mail, Pastor J. Martin, Calvary Community Church, Phoenix, Arizona, www.calvaryphx.com

28. Streams in the Desert, L.B. Cowan, September 19

29. Grace Mail, Pastor J. Martin, Calvary Community Church, Phoenix, Arizona, www.calvaryphx.com

30. Daniel Crawford, author

31. Mark Guy Pearse, author

32. Grace Mail, Pastor J. Martin, Calvary Community Church, Phoenix, Arizona, www.calvaryphx.com

33. Victorious Christian Living, Alan Redpath, p. 166

CPSIA information can be obtained at www.ICGtesting.com
Printed in the USA
BVOW04s1129250814

364142BV00004B/7/P